A BOY FROM ACADIE
ROMÉO LEBLANC'S JOURNEY TO RIDEAU HALL

Beryl Young

BOUTON D'OR ACADIE

A BOY FROM ACADIE

For its publishing activities, Bouton d'or Acadie acknowledges the financial support of the Province of New Brunswick, the Canada Council for the Arts and the Government of Canada through the Canada Book Fund.

Title: A Boy from Acadie. Roméo LeBlanc's Journey to Rideau Hall
Author: Beryl Young
Illustrations: Maurice Cormier
Editing: Jo-Anne Elder
Literary Director: Sébastien Lord-Émard
Graphic Design: atelier46
Printing: Transcontinental

ISBN 978-2-89750-125-9
ISBN (PDF) 978-2-89750-126-6
Copyright © 2018 Beryl Young and Bouton d'or Acadie
Library and Archives Canada

This book is also available in eBook format

Distributed in French by Prologue
Phone 1-800-363-2864
Fax 1-800-361-8088
Email prologue@prologue.ca

Distributed by Nimbus Publishing
P.O. Box 9166, Halifax, NS B3K 5M8
Phone: 1-800-646-2879
Fax: 902-455-5440
Email: customerservice@nimbus.ca

Bouton d'or Acadie
PO Box 575, Moncton (NB) E1C 8L9 Canada
Phone: 1-506-382-1367
Fax: 1-506-854-7577
Email: boutondoracadie@nb.aibn.com
www.boutondoracadie.com

Created in Acadie. Printed in Canada

This book is dedicated to the family of Roméo LeBlanc
and to my new Acadian friends.

Ottawa

CANADA

Maritime Provinces
Acadie

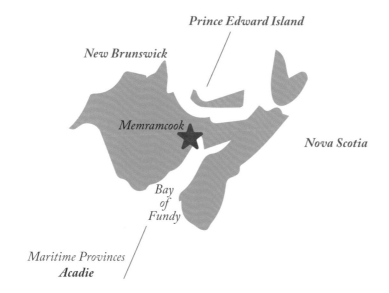

Prince Edward Island

New Brunswick

Memramcook

Nova Scotia

Bay
of
Fundy

Maritime Provinces
Acadie

INTRODUCTION

Never in a million years would an Acadian boy growing up on a small farm in New Brunswick dream that one day he would meet the queen and become her representative in the highest position in his country.

But that is the true story of a Canadian boy named Roméo.

It's the story of the youngest of seven children who would never have gone on to high school without the help of his sister sending money from her work as a maid. The story of how the boy's hard work and love of learning led to scholarships for study at the Sorbonne in Paris.

This book tells how Roméo LeBlanc came to serve with three prime ministers, how he worked to protect Canadian fishing rights, and then became governor general of Canada.

This boy, who loved the Acadian custom of dipping bread into the molasses on the underside of his plate, would one day be comfortable dining with Queen Elizabeth II in Sandringham House.

I am honoured to tell the inspiring story of how a man of humble origins became the first Acadian governor general of Canada, Roméo Adrien LeBlanc.

The elementary school Roméo attended in Cormier's Cove

CHAPTER 1
SCHOOL AT LAST

When you are six years old, the first day of school is the most exciting day in the world.

As the youngest child in the LeBlanc family, Roméo had to wait. He watched impatiently as his six brothers and sisters started school, one after the other. Waiting for them to come home made the days long for Roméo. But in the evenings, his sister Alice would let him sit next to her and turn the pages of her books. The bright little boy was learning a great deal before he even started school.

Roméo lived with his large family in Cormier's Cove, near the village of Memramcook. Their farm was part of a small Acadian community not far from the Bay of Fundy in New Brunswick. Like other Acadians, they were Catholic and spoke French, and their ancestors had come from France to settle in the New World, in a community that became known as "Acadie."

Roméo's father, Philéas, worked at the busy Canadian National Railway work yards in nearby Moncton.

Finally, when he was almost six years old, in September of 1933, the great day came when Roméo could start school.

With his heart beating hard in excitement, he walked along the trail to the small village school with his sister Alice, who was ten, and his brother Léonard, who was eight.

From the very first day Roméo loved the school, with its big black coal stove in the middle of the room, the desks in rows around it. For the first three years, his teacher was nineteen-year-old Miss Dorilla Blanchet. She was only five feet tall with blond curly hair and a welcoming smile. There were fifty-seven children and seven grades in her classroom!

Roméo was so excited he'd arrive early in the morning to help Miss Blanchet. The job he liked was smacking the chalk out of the blackboard brushes. At lunchtime he ate bread and molasses sandwiches packed by his mother and his oldest sister Irène, who was twenty.

Many of his schoolmates had the same last name as he did, LeBlanc. They were all descended from Daniel LeBlanc, one of the early Acadian settlers from France.

THE ACADIAN STORY AND THE DEPORTATION

Roméo LeBlanc was a direct descendant of Daniel LeBlanc, who travelled from France in 1645 to a colony in North America. The settlers shared the land with the Mi'kmaq people in the Maritimes, a land they proudly called Acadie.

The Acadian settlers established themselves in this rich new land as farmers and fishermen. Their colony grew steadily and maintained a distinct identity and culture. For years Acadians lived peacefully amid the beautiful valleys and the balsam firs, through warm summers and snowy winters.

By 1713 the British and the French had both established colonies in North America. Reflecting the war in Europe, there were frequent clashes between them. The Treaty of Utrecht, signed that year, gave most of Acadie to the British Empire.

In 1755, Colonel Charles Lawrence, fighting for British control of the land, demanded that the Acadian people sign an oath of allegiance to Britain. The Acadians, who wanted to remain neutral, would not take up arms against the French and refused to sign. The British authorities in Halifax gave an order to deport them. This meant sending Acadians away from their own land and scattering them throughout the New England Colonies in what was to become part of the United States. As many as 10,000 Acadians were shipped away. Families were often split up and their lands taken over by the British. Sadly, for almost ten years Acadians lived as refugees torn away from their beloved land.

In 1763 the French and British ended their war with the Peace Treaty of Paris, and soon after, the Acadians were allowed to return. Some went to France, some chose to stay in the United

States, and some returned to make new homes in Nova Scotia, New Brunswick and Prince Edward Island, as the territories that were once part of Acadie were now called. They worked hard, and their numbers and their culture flourished once again. Acadians were not given the right to vote until fifty years later.

Today, the Acadian people make up almost a third of the population of New Brunswick and live in places all over the world.

His new friend Laurianne LeBlanc, who was two years older than Roméo, had a seat beside him on the wooden bench by the window. When the cold weather came, the students sitting close to the big boiler were too hot. Next to the windows, Laurianne and Roméo were freezing.

Laurianne remembers Roméo well, and says, "We were good friends, even though he was younger than I was. He was so lively. He wasn't afraid to speak out and always had his hand up to answer the teacher's questions."

In the spring Roméo watched the older boys play baseball, practising at home to throw the ball and asking a neighbour to play catch with him. On Saturday afternoons there were radio broadcasts of the New York Yankees baseball game. Roméo's hero was Joe DiMaggio who was making a reputation for himself as the high-hitting batsman on the Yankee team.

After school Roméo would rush home to tell his mother about his day. She was usually sitting on the sofa. She looked tired, with her dark hair falling out of the bun tied at the back of her head. She smiled at him, her youngest boy, not big for his age but full of energy and mischief. Roméo was glad to see her smile. She often looked sad, and Roméo knew why. He could barely remember Raoul, the baby brother who had died when Roméo was three. It seemed as though one day there was a baby in the house, crying all the time, then the baby was gone and the house was too quiet.

Roméo's parents, Philéas and Lucie LeBlanc

Mama has bad headaches, Irène told Roméo. Try to be quiet.

Irène and Émilie had stopped going to school after Grade 7 to help their mother keep house for the younger children as well as their deaf grandfather who lived with the family. Eighteen-year-old Antoine had stopped school too and was working on the farm. Roméo's sister Valéda was boarding at a convent school.

Roméo's sisters took over the big job of cooking whenever their mother had one of her frequent headaches. There were meals to cook and loaves of bread to bake in the wood stove. The LeBlanc family may have been poor, but they always had good food. They grew vegetables on the farm, and ate cod and salmon caught in the nearby Petitcodiac River. Best of all, Roméo loved the fat sausages they sometimes had for lunch. He always ate everything on his plate, except for the green peas. Even when the peas were fresh from the farm garden, Roméo couldn't stand the taste of them!

When the family had eaten their meal, they would turn their plates over and pour molasses inside the bottom rim of the plate. It was the Acadian custom to dip bread into molasses for dessert.

When she could, his mother made *fricot* for dinner. She put a big pot on the stove and filled it with broth, vegetables, and chicken or fish, always fresh savoury herb and sometimes dumplings. This was an Acadian specialty and was often served with samphire greens that Roméo and Alice gathered in the salt marsh by the Memramcook River. Steamed samphire greens were delicious. They tasted just like asparagus.

Roméo's first year of school went by quickly and Miss Blanchet passed him into the next grade. "He's a smart little fellow," she told his parents. Roméo was very happy to learn that Miss Blanchet would be his teacher again the next year.

Roméo had to pitch in and help around the farm in the summer. Even though he was the youngest, he was expected to do his share, and the chores seemed endless. There was water to bring in from the well, constant weeding in the big garden, and piles of wood to stack. Every day the cows, pigs, and chickens had to be fed.

His brother Léonard was in charge of rounding up the cows at night, and he'd make Roméo come with him. Roméo hung back at the edge of the field, scared of the cows, but even more scared of the bull. It looked so big and mean. Léonard, who loved all the work around the farm, especially the animals, didn't understand his brother and was impatient with him.

One day in late summer Léonard sent Roméo out alone to bring in the cows. Roméo came back and reported that the cows weren't in the field. "They're just not there," he said, trying to convince his brother. Alarmed, Léonard rushed to the field to find that the cows were definitely there. And so was the bull!

"Roméo's hopeless!" Léonard reported to his parents.

The only chore Roméo seemed to like was picking berries with his sisters, and of course he loved everything about school.

Cover of the 1905 Le Petit Larousse "Je sème à tout vent"

- GROWING UP -

In September, Roméo was excited to be back at school with Miss Blanchet, Laurianne, and his other friends. They all spoke French and the subjects were taught in French, but the text books supplied by the province were in English. Only their story books were in French.

Roméo always worked quickly and usually finished his lessons ahead of the others in the class. When Roméo finished early, Miss Blanchet let him spend time poring over the well-worn class book, Le Petit Larousse. This thick book was a dictionary combined with an encyclopedia. It was full of interesting pictures and new words to learn. The motto of the 1905 school edition was *Je sème à tout vent* which translates as "I sow to all winds." Indeed, that book opened up the world for the young school boy.

Many Acadian men in the area were were employed
at the Canadian National railway work yards in Moncton

Sometimes Roméo and his friends went to watch the freight trains loaded with salt cod heading west. They were told the cod was being sent to the Canadian prairies where the farmers used the fish to patch the roofs on their houses. Roméo was astonished. They *ate* the salt cod in New Brunswick! People in all parts of Canada were suffering in the Depression and the cod was being sent to the prairies for food, but the gift had back-fired because most prairie people found it too salty to eat.

Another time, Roméo was walking with his friends to the Rockland Bridge, a long covered bridge nearby, and when they reached the railway track Roméo lay down and put his ear to one of the rails. "That's a dumb thing to do," his friends said. Roméo insisted that he just wanted to hear when a train was coming.

"Trains come all the time," they yelled, pulling Roméo up. "You're crazy," they told him. "You'll get yourself killed."

But Roméo was fascinated by the trains that came from the larger world beyond the village. Little did he know the same train would take him out into that big world one day, away from the village and his family.

When winter came and deep snow piled up on the slopes near the school, Roméo was the first one outdoors at recess. He had his own little sled, and never got tired of whizzing down the hills, over and over again.

At the end of Roméo's second year, Miss Blanchet wrote that Roméo was a pleasure to teach. He was good in all subjects, and at the head of his class.

Roméo's oldest sister Irène had always taken special care of Roméo. Now with their mother still feeling sad about the baby's death, it was Irène who made Roméo's favourite buckwheat pancakes for breakfast. She saw him off to school and made sure he had his lunch.

But change was coming. Irène had fallen in love with a local farmer, who came courting in an Acadian ritual called *la grande demande*. The family prepared for the suitor by making special sandwiches. It was the only occasion when the crusts were cut off the bread. However, when the suitor came to the house, the family discovered that the tray of sandwiches had disappeared! Roméo had eaten them, somehow hoping that having no sandwiches would put Irène's suitor off. Instead, Roméo got into trouble and Irène's romance blossomed. Within months she was married and had moved to live on her husband's farm. Roméo missed her desperately and always called her his "second mother."

THE STORY OF EVANGELINE

The famous poem called *Evangeline, A Tale of Acadie* (1847) was written by Henry Wadsworth Longfellow. It tells the heartbreaking story of a young Acadian woman who is separated from her lover, Gabriel, during the Deportation. Evangeline spends many years searching for Gabriel,but does not find him until they have both grown old and Gabriel is on his deathbed. The statue is located in Grand Pré, Nova Scotia, where many of the Acadian people were put on ships to leave their lands.

CHAPTER 2
SAD DAYS
FOR THE FAMILY

Over the next school year, the family became more and more alarmed that their mother suffered with so many headaches. Roméo would rush home from school to find his mother sitting on the sofa, her head in her hands. He sat beside her and tried to make her feel better by reading from one of his school books.

But one day in February, Roméo came home and his mother was not on the sofa. His father was home and he put his arms around Roméo. "Your Maman died this morning," he said quietly.

Roméo was eight years old and it felt like the end of the world. Why did she die? Parents only die when they are old. His mother wasn't old.

Roméo's mother, Lucie LeBlanc

Irène sat on the sofa beside Roméo. She told him the doctor said Maman had probably died of high blood pressure. She was only forty-nine. Roméo sobbed until he was too exhausted to cry any more.

His mother's body lay in the bedroom, and their father took the children into the room to say *au revoir*. Roméo's sisters held their heartbroken little brother as he wept.

Alice sewed black mourning bands on her brother's jackets, and for the next two days, visitors came to pay their respects to the family. Friends from Roméo's class arrived to visit him after school, but when they got to the house, Roméo was nowhere to be seen. He was hiding under his bed and wouldn't come out. The miserable boy didn't want his friends to see him cry.

Things were changing quickly in the family. Émilie had left home a few months earlier, when she was just sixteen. She had found work as a maid with a family near Boston in the United States. Roméo only saw her twice a year, when she came home for the holidays. So it was necessary for his sister Valéda, who was enjoying school at the nearby convent, to leave school and come home to help in the house.

Antoine and Léonard ran the farm, and Alice was busy helping Valéda in the kitchen. Léonard was constantly frustrated with Roméo, who disliked farm work as much as ever. The whole family missed their mother, but no one more than her youngest son.

The Reds of Sixty-Nine

We used no mattress on our hands,
No cage upon our face;
We stood right up and caught the ball,
With courage and with grace.
— Harry Ellard (1880s)

- MORE BASEBALL -

That spring was a very unhappy time for Roméo, but his friends at school understood and were kind to him. He was old enough now to play baseball with the bigger boys. For hours at a time, they played ball in a cow pasture behind the school, using potato sacks to mark the bases.

Their old bat was held together with tape and glue. Running to a base sometimes meant sliding through the muck of one of the wet cow patties scattered over the field. They didn't always have enough boys for two teams, so everyone played more than one position. Roméo's favourite position was catcher. He didn't have a mask to protect his face or a glove to make catching easier.

One day a batter swung the bat and hit Roméo right in his face. He was taken to a doctor with a broken nose. When he got home again, Roméo told Alice that the doctor was mean. He'd grabbed hold of Roméo's nose, jerked it back into shape, and sent him home. The next day, Roméo was back at the baseball field.

It was during those years that Roméo grew even more passionate about big league baseball. The New York Yankee games were broadcast on the radio every Saturday afternoon and Roméo tried to listen to every one. He'd sit cross-legged on the floor by the big radio in the family living room to cheer his champion, Joe DiMaggio, who was continuing to make amazing hits.

When Roméo moved on to Grade 4, a teacher from another school boarded with the LeBlanc family. This was a great opportunity for Roméo; he had a teacher right in his own house! He could eat meals with her, and in the evenings ask questions about his school work. More chances to learn all the things that fascinated the curious boy. At night they'd sit side by side at the kitchen table with the glow from a single kerosene lamp falling over the school books.

One Sunday in the summer, Roméo went with his friend Laurianne to pick blueberries in a field near Taylor village, the English-speaking community two miles away. Roméo's own Catholic family went to Mass on Sunday mornings and now it seemed strange to hear hymns being sung in the afternoon at the Protestant Baptist church.

Laurianne and Roméo picked berries all day. Roméo had picked seven boxes and Laurianne had picked twelve. The pay from an English employer was set at one cent a box, but Valéda came to meet them and argued with the boss. "You should be paying two cents a box," she told him. The man finally agreed. So Laurianne earned twenty-four cents and Roméo made fourteen cents. That was a lot of money in those days. They were rich.

With the huge sum of fourteen cents in his pocket, Roméo walked to the general store in Memramcook. The store was alongside the imposing building that was St. Joseph's College. He bought bubble gum for one cent a pack. The pack included a hockey card with the picture of a hockey player. Roméo loved collecting the cards, and he loved chewing gum. Never in school, of course.

When he turned eleven, Roméo got a summer job on the dikes, working as a timekeeper with the men who repaired the dikes. The dikes had been built to prevent the *grande marée*, the tidal salt water of the distant Bay of Fundy, from flooding the nearby fields. Roméo's job was to signal the workers when it was time to open the flood gates and let the water through.

Photo of dike

For the next two years of school, Grade 6 and 7, Roméo's life outside school was busy. Almost every day in the winter the boys played hockey on the marsh ice. His friend who was the goalie would stuff thick Eaton's catalogues in his socks for leg pads. In the summer they played baseball in the field behind the school. And there was always work on the farm under Léonard's supervision. Whenever he could, Roméo would sneak away to read one of his books. Léonard would find him and put him back to work.

Every Saturday Léonard sent Alice and Roméo out to weed the garden plot in the hot sun. The weeding seemed endless. Roméo made a fuss and scuffed his feet in the dirt. "It takes too long. I'll miss the baseball game on the radio," he told Alice. She grinned at her brother and whispered, "Stop complaining. I have an idea,"

Quietly and deliberately she showed her brother how to leave the weeds and pull out the carrot and beet tops. growing young learner and his sister's Roméo was a quick Léonard came to plan worked. When and saw the mess Roméo inspect the garden good plants with the had made, tearing up announced that he'd never weeds still thriving, he let him loose in the garden again. Just what Roméo wanted to hear!

He grinned at Alice and rushed off to catch the last half of the baseball game. After the game, Roméo stayed out of Léonard's way, grabbed a piece of fudge from the kitchen and escaped with his book.

Roméo was happiest when he was in school. Every teacher liked his wide interests and his enthusiasm for learning. He was never shy and not afraid to speak up in class. Perhaps this came from being the youngest in the family. He always volunteered for *récitations*, recitals where students recited poems learned by heart in front of their schoolmates. At Christmas, the school put on a show and Roméo always had a part. His family attended and clapped loudly for their little brother, who was so outgoing and confident.

There had been rumours of war in Europe, and at the start of the next school year, in 1939, war was declared by Britain and France against Hitler's Germany. Europe seemed far away, but the radio was full of the news that Germany had invaded France. Little did Roméo know that in a very few years he would be a student himself in France at the famed Sorbonne university.

French books used in Roméo's classes

In his last year of elementary school, there was a new teacher all the students liked. She had threatened to leave unless the school board paid her more money. It was a cold winter and the teacher agreed to settle for a warm winter coat that would cost six dollars. A trustee went around to the parents in the district, asking each household for twenty-five cents for the coat. All the families paid, including Roméo's, and the popular teacher, dressed in her warm new coat, stayed on as the teacher.

That year, there was a story in the class reader entitled "A Mother's Heart." Roméo read about a young girl learning her mother has died. The heartbroken girl kneels sobbing beside her mother's bed, her tears falling on her mother's chest. In the story, the girl suddenly hears her mother's heart begin to beat again. Her tears have brought her dear mother back to life.

Poor Roméo. He put his head down on the school desk. He had cried and cried when his mother died, but she hadn't come back to life. The story made him miss his mother more than ever.

Roméo's school years came to an end when he graduated from Grade 7. Roméo's father had always said that was enough schooling for children. Philéas had never learned to read or write himself and his children were needed to help on the farm.

Roméo had to accept the fact that all his sisters and brothers had stopped school at Grade 7 and there would be no more school for him, either. Even his good friend Laurianne had left school two years earlier and was now beginning to earn a living as a dressmaker in the village.

Roméo resigned himself to baseball and his reading when he could squeeze them into the busy days working on the farm.

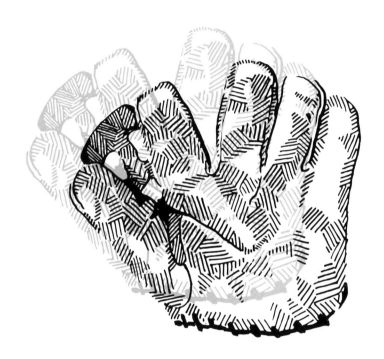

St. Joseph's College in Memramcook

CHAPTER 3
NO MORE SCHOOL

The long summer of farm work was over. Roméo had spent every day in August with his father cutting down spruce trees on the farm to sell as firewood. The wood had to be chopped and loaded onto a wagon. It was hard work. Roméo could feel his legs growing stronger and there were new muscles on his arms. In some ways it was good to be fit and active after the winter of sitting at a school desk, but he was starting to feel bored. Was this what he'd be doing the rest of his life?

In September some of his friends from Cormier's Cove had started high school in Moncton, over thirty kilometers away. For Roméo, it was time to hitch the horses to the wagon and go with his father to take the chopped wood into Memramcook. The first load was destined for the largest building, St. Joseph's College, run by the Holy Cross Fathers. It offered three years of high school as well as four years to complete a university degree.

Roméo's father drove the horses to a large shed at the back of the brick building. He motioned for Roméo to get down and start unloading the wood. For almost an hour they worked to pile the wood in the shed.

The back door of the college opened, and Father Superior Lapalme came out, ready to pay Roméo's father for the wood. The payment had nothing to do with Roméo, so he reached for the book he'd been reading and jumped up onto the wagon. He barely listened as his father talked to the priest.

Père Lapalme asked why the boy wasn't in school.

Philéas answered, "My son finished school in June. He's needed to help around the farm."

"He's got his nose in a book. Seems like a bright boy," Père Lapalme said.

Philéas answered. "Roméo's always reading. He'll soon get used to hard work."

Père Lapalme shrugged his shoulders. "That seems a shame," he said. "The boy might be a good student."

At this, Roméo finally looked up and stared at the tall building, with its long rows of windows on five floors. Classrooms, teachers, books.

Père Lapalme must have seen the longing on Roméo's face, and he leaned closer to Roméo's father, trying to persuade him. "The college students learn English. It's important for getting on in the world."

Roméo's father didn't answer.

Père Lapalme tried again, making an offer. "Tell you what," he said. "If you give the college that winter's load of wood, St. Joseph's will give your boy a year's free tuition."

Roméo's father shook his head, saying, "*Merci*, no. All my sons work on our farm."

Père Lapalme looked at Roméo's father. "Think about it," he told him. "It's a fair deal for you and an opportunity for your boy."

Roméo was really listening now.

Philéas looked right back at Père Lapalme. "I won't change my mind," he said firmly.

Père Lapalme said he understood and handed over the money for the load of wood.

As they drove away, Roméo put his head down, his eyes stinging so sharply he couldn't pick up his book to read.

Philéas LeBlanc, Roméo's father

- ÉMILIE DECIDES TO HELP -

As the weeks passed, Roméo didn't think too much about his missed opportunity. His father set the rules in their family. At age twelve, you obeyed them.

Roméo worked every day around the farm, hoeing the turnips needed for cattle feed, cutting wood and handling the cows, always on the watch for the big bull. Each day it became clearer in his mind that he wasn't like Antoine and Léonard. They enjoyed farm work. He never would.

The autumn went on, and the family looked forward to Émilie coming home for Thanksgiving weekend. Émilie arrived, full of stories about her life as a maid in Boston. She made them all laugh with funny tales about the family she worked for.

Valéda and Alice did their best to prepare a good meal for their family. They cooked a big pot of chicken *fricot*, the dish their mother made for special occasions. At the dinner table, Émilie asked how everyone was doing. Somehow it came up that, earlier in September, the Father Superior at St. Joseph's had offered Roméo a place in Grade 8 at the college.

When Émilie heard that her father had said no to the offer, she put down her spoon and looked across the table. "Papa, I don't understand. Why would you would deny Roméo the chance to get more education?"

Philéas continued eating.

Émilie spoke again. "Roméo's the smartest one in our family. He should get this chance. A chance to get out into the world instead of being stuck on the farm."

Their father shook his head. "A high school education just trains boys to be clerks and lawyers. I want my sons to stay honest. Not just be out for money."

At this point, Alice spoke up. "If Maman were here," she said, "She would want Roméo to go to high school."

Philéas looked solemn, and everyone around the table was quiet. It was true. Maman had pushed for Valéda to have more schooling at the convent, but then Valéda had to leave the convent to help at home after her mother died.

The subject of Roméo going to high school was dropped and the meal continued.

Émilie lay awake in bed all night. The boys in the American family she worked for would all go to high school. Roméo should have that opportunity too. Look how well he'd done in school, how his teachers had praised his work and said he was so smart! It was obvious that he didn't fit into farm life.

The next morning, she'd made a decision. She would use her own money to pay Roméo's tuition at the college. Her father couldn't stop her.

Philéas didn't put up much of a fight. Antoine and Léonard were still at home to help. Before too long they would marry and bring their wives to live on the farm. Soon there would be children and more hands to help with the work. Perhaps the reminder about his beloved wife made him think differently about Roméo.

Émilie didn't have much money saved. Before she left for her job across the border, she arranged with the college to pay Roméo's fees in instalments throughout the year.

Roméo would be the first one in his family to attend high school. It would be thanks to his sister, working as a maid in an American home.

CHAPTER 4
GIFT FROM A SISTER

It was more than two months into the school year, but Roméo was excited to be going into Grade 8. He would be thirteen in December. He was small and skinny for his age, but he was ready to learn.

The LeBlanc farm was over five kilometers from Memramcook, too far to walk every day, so Roméo had to board with a family in the village. It was a strange experience to be living away from his own family. Even the food was different. His landlady served peanut butter almost every day and Roméo had never liked it. And when she served green peas, he pushed them to the side of his plate.

But Roméo loved being in high school. It was wonderful to learn new things. Father Goguen, one of Roméo's teachers, took Roméo under his wing and helped him adjust to the big school. "It's important to learn English," he told him. "It will stand you in good stead in the future." Father Goguen was right.

School had always been easy for Roméo, but he discovered that one of the college classes was surprisingly hard. It was French—the language he'd spoken all his life, the language used by the teachers in his elementary school. But they had never taught grammar or spelling. It came as a big shock on his first French test, when Roméo discovered he'd made thirty-two mistakes!

He'd have to work harder at French, as well as keep up with his classes in arithmetic, geography, and history, and for the first time, study English.

Roméo was never afraid of this kind of work, and it paid off. Every week at St. Joseph's, he gained new confidence in his own abilities.

The first year went by quickly. During that time there were more big changes in the family. Valéda had recently married and moved to live with her husband on his farm. Émilie was still far away in Massachusetts. Alice, Léonard, and Antoine were at home, but now Antoine had married too. He brought his bride Mélindé, a local girl who was just eighteen, to live at the LeBlanc family farm. She helped Alice in the kitchen and was already a good cook. Like his sisters, Mélindé spoiled Roméo and she quickly became another "mother" to him.

Because of the war, sugar, molasses and butter were rationed, but Mélindé saved up her food coupons to make special treats for the family. She found a way to cook "Pudding in a bag," a delicious mix of flour, sugar and suet or butter, rolled into a ball. A hole made in the ball was filled with raisins, apples and cinnamon. Roméo loved the steamed dessert.

POUTINE À TROU OR PUDDING IN A BAG

Makes 12 poutines.
Roméo loved this treat.

Ingredients

PASTRY
2 1/2 cups flour
4 teaspoons baking powder
½ teaspoon salt
2 tablespoons sugar
¼ cup butter
¾ cup milk

FILLING
4 apples, peeled and cut in small pieces
½ cup or more raisins
½ cup cranberries

SYRUP
1 cup brown sugar
¾ cup water

Directions

1. Sift flour, baking powder, salt and sugar and blend in butter to form a coarse mixture.

2. Add milk and mix dough well. Divide into twelve pieces.

3. Roll each piece to a circle 5-6 inches wide

4. Place apples, raisins and cranberries in the centre of each dough circle

5. Moisten the edges of the dough with milk or water and roll the dough around the ingredients to make a ball

6. Leave a small opening in the top and place on a pan

7. Bake at 350 degrees for 30 minutes or until golden brown

8. Make the syrup by mixing the brown sugar and water, and boil for 5 minutes.

9. Pour the syrup into the hole on the top of each poutine. Makes 12 poutines.

Every weekend Roméo walked home to the farm, bringing his laundry. After months of nagging and pushing Roméo to take on more work, Léonard was coming to accept things. Roméo's heart would never be in farm work, Léonard realized. His brother might be smart, but he would always be completely useless around the farm.

Alice, who was frustrated that she hadn't been able to find a job, still worked hard alongside Roméo, with Léonard supervising to make sure they were picking weeds instead of edible plants.

Like many young people in the 1940's, Alice had started smoking. Roméo kept pestering his sister until she gave in and handed Roméo his first cigarette. They'd sneak away together and smoke whenever they could get out of farm chores. When he was an adult, Roméo always joked that his sister Alice had taught him to smoke, but admitted he later came to his senses and gave up the habit.

In the summer Émilie came home for her two-week summer holiday. The family where she worked had a boy who was two years older than Roméo, and she brought back second-hand clothes the boy had outgrown. What became Roméo's prize possession was a brown houndstooth tweed jacket. It was a bit too big for him and so flashy it was hard to miss. With the jacket came a pair of saddle shoes, brown and white, unlike anything seen in the village. They had come from his big sister, and Roméo wore them with pride. He loved having Émilie around and was always sad when her short holidays ended, and she had to go back to Boston.

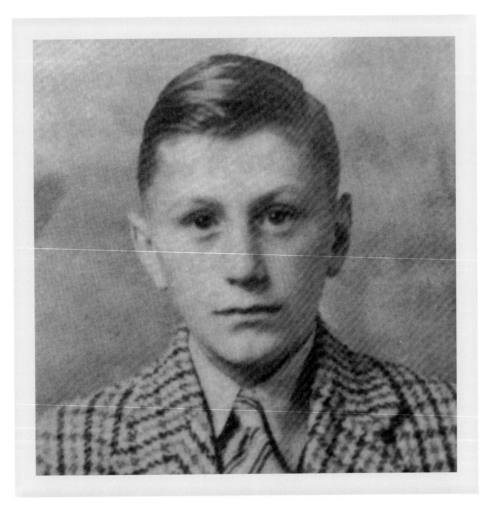

Roméo proudly wearing his houndstooth jacket

Later that year there was one more big change in Roméo's life. Alice had tried hard but she couldn't find work in Memramcook so she decided to join her sister in the United States. She found a job as a maid in the small town near where Émilie worked. Now she'd be able to help Émilie pay Roméo's school fees. But now Alice was far away too, and Roméo missed the sister who made him laugh and taught him to play tricks.

As his high school years went on, Roméo made many friends and became a popular boy who loved sports. There was a marsh behind the school, and when it froze it was time for ice hockey. When the weather was warmer the boys played baseball for hours on a field beside the college. Roméo was known as a fast runner.

Over the spring and summer of 1941, Joe DiMaggio had his famous fifty-six game hitting streak, a record that had helped the New York Yankees win nine world championships. Day after day, along with everyone else in the country, Roméo was glued to the radio as the hitting record was being set. He had a dream that one day he might see his hero take the bat at home plate.

Roméo (on right) with friends as a Boy Scout

Roméo and the other college students were too young to sign up to fight in the war, but he had joined a Boy Scout group and went camping with them on nearby Lac St-Camille.

New Brunswick played an important role during the war being fought in Europe. Not far from Memramcook there was a large Air Force training base, where pilots and crew from around the world trained for war service. The village boys were thrilled every time the noisy Harvard and Anson bombers made their low flights over the village.

Almost every week, trains full of Canadian soldiers sped by on the railway close to the college. Roméo went with the other boys to stand at the tracks and wave to the troops heading to Halifax where they would board ships to fight overseas.

The next two years went by quickly as Roméo grew physically and intellectually, thriving in the busy life at St. Joseph's. The more his teachers challenged him, the harder he worked.

In Roméo's third year of high school, his sister Émilie fell in love and married a U.S. serviceman. Freddie Gallant was also an Acadian, a descendent of the Acadians who had stayed in the United States after the deportation. Émilie and her new husband decided to do something special for Roméo. Something to make his wildest dream come true.

JOE DIMAGGIO'S BASEBALL CAREER

Joe DiMaggio was born in 1914, in California, and had eight brothers and sisters. His Sicilian father wanted Joe to work with him as a fisherman, but Joe discovered he couldn't stand the smell of fish. He decided to practise playing ball, hoping he'd make the big league in baseball.

Joe's hard work paid off, and at twenty-five he was a star hitter with the New York Yankees. His big year as a record batter was in the summer of 1941 when Joltin' Joe, as he was called, achieved the impossible, breaking the former record of 41 winning games.

That summer, the tension grew game after game as Joe hit a series of home runs and long balls. Cheered on by 31,000 fans, his hitting streak went on for 20 games! 30 games! He broke the record at 41 games! Joe kept on hitting and made an unbelievable all-time high of 56 games! Both sides of the stadium cheered wildly. So did fans across North America listening on their radios. Joe's record hits took the Yankees team on a winning streak and made newspaper headlines all over the country.

Always a modest man, Joe said he was amazed at his good luck. He'd always said you could accomplish great things if you worked hard.

Later Joe DiMaggio was named to the Baseball Hall of Fame. During his career Joe hit 361 home runs and had over 1,500 runs batted in.

- A SURPRISE TRIP -

Émilie had told Freddie how crazy her brother was about Joe DiMaggio, so she and Freddie sent Roméo his first baseball glove. Roméo was thrilled. The glove was real leather. Then Émilie and Freddie announced another surprise. They were sending Roméo a bus ticket to New York to see Joe DiMaggio play baseball.

Roméo couldn't believe it!

The trip was planned for the school holidays in July. He would visit Émilie and Freddie near Boston, and then he would go on to New York. If he made it to Yankee Stadium he might be lucky and see his hero.

Roméo had never dreamed that a sixteen-year-old from a small village in New Brunswick could go on a trip like this. First there was an eight-hour bus trip through Maine and Vermont, before he arrived at the apartment where Émilie and her husband lived. For a few days Émilie had a chance to spoil her little brother. She took him to the biggest candy store Roméo had ever seen, with rows of every kind of candy he could imagine.

After two days, Émilie put him on another bus headed to New York City. Roméo watched from the bus window, amazed at the size of the big farms in the lush Connecticut countryside. Finally, on the outskirts of New York City, the bus passed rows of tall buildings before it stopped at the large central bus station.

One of the priests at St. Joseph's had arranged for Roméo to stay in a New York seminary. But when finally found the seminary there was no room for him, so a priest took him to a nearby basement apartment. Alone in a dark room in the largest city in the world, Roméo was scared to death. He kept the light on and wouldn't let himself fall asleep.

With the morning light, New York wasn't so frightening, but Roméo had to find out how to get to Yankee stadium. He asked a stranger for help and learned which city bus to take. At last Roméo found the large stadium and bought a ticket for a seat far up in the stands. Baseball cap on his head, crunching from a box of Crackerjacks he bought for five cents, the young fan watched his hero Joe DiMaggio pick up his special bat and walk to home plate. Joe's record batting streak had ended two years earlier, but he was still playing brilliantly, and Roméo saw his hero win the game for his team. Roméo had borrowed a Brownie camera and took a whole roll of photographs, even one of home plate. It was blurry and far away, but the memory of his hero standing beside it would always be crystal clear.

HIGH SCHOOL GRADUATION,
AND ANOTHER SURPRISE

Back at St. Joseph's there was more hard work for Roméo's final year. Roméo was seventeen when he completed high school, and near the top of his class, second in English and calligraphy and surprisingly, first in French. He didn't do so well in mathematics.

The graduation ceremony was held in the college auditorium and the students lined up to be given a handshake and their graduation certificate. Roméo opened his certificate in front of his proud family. It was a blank piece of paper!

There was a problem with his school fees. Émilie and Alice had done their best, but they hadn't been able to make the last payment.

Roméo studying at college

CHAPTER 5
ON TO UNIVERSITY

Roméo had been such an excellent student that his teachers at St. Joseph's encouraged him to study for a Bachelor of Arts degree. It was what Roméo wanted to do, but there was the matter of his unpaid fees. Roméo's graduation from high school didn't became official until a few weeks later when Émilie and Alice could make the final payment.

The college offered some financial help for Roméo's university tuition, and his sisters would keep sending money from their modest salaries, but Roméo's father would have to help too. Philéas had come to accept that his son would never be suited for farm life. In place of helping with the tuition, he sent eggs and garden vegetables to the college.

Roméo made his own contribution; he found three jobs. He was on duty to answer the college phone, he worked in the college library and he helped serve meals to the priests at the long tables in the dining room. With all these jobs and his university courses, Roméo often didn't have enough time to go home on the weekends.

The university students came from all over New Brunswick as well as Quebec and the U.S. They slept in a large dormitory where a bell rang every morning at 6:30 for Mass, followed by breakfast. The boys were in the classrooms by 8:15 a.m., ready to start on the heavy curriculum. They studied Latin, Greek, religion, mathematics, history, economics, philosophy, and science, as well as French and English literature and language.

The students read the works of Shakespeare, Dickens, and Molière. They wrote weekly essays and had debates in English as well as French. They listened to classical music and acted in plays. Roméo loved it all, but it was getting harder to squeeze in time for baseball games.

The world was opening up for Roméo, and it was very exciting. In his second year of university in 1945, World War II came to an end. The students tossed their caps in the air, joining the villagers who streamed out onto the streets to celebrate. It was a hard victory; over seventeen million Allied soldiers had died. Among them were nine young men from Memramcook.

The future of Europe was being debated around the world, and at the college too, but the college subscribed to only one copy of the French newspaper *Le Devoir*. Every morning the paper was opened and posted on the bulletin board and the students crowded around to read pages one and two. In the afternoon the paper was turned to pages three and four. Roméo and his friends had heated debates about world affairs. At that time, Roméo had no idea that journalism would become his first career.

When he had longer holidays, Roméo stayed on the farm. His father and Léonard were there, along with Antoine and Mélindé who now had two children. Valéda lived away with her family, and Alice and Émilie were still working in the United States. Roméo tried to help Léonard and Antoine with the farm work, but they both knew Roméo preferred reading his textbooks to milking cows and chopping wood. As Roméo looked around the dinner table he couldn't help but compare his own clean hands with the rough and dirt-encrusted hands of his hard-working brothers. His life with books and papers was a long way from the soil on the farm. In a way, he had let his brothers and his father down by abandoning the farm to go to university.

Mélindé was busy cooking for everyone and to make Roméo feel useful, she suggested he help around the kitchen. She bribed him with a promise of baking his favourite chocolate brownies to take back to the college. The bribe worked. Roméo peeled potatoes and washed dishes in exchange for Mélindé's brownies. The only problem was the brownies had to be shared with the other students once he was back in the dormitory!

In his last two years Roméo was editor of the student newspaper *Liaisons*. He wrote impassioned editorials encouraging Acadians not to forget their history and to respect their own culture. Throughout his life he credited the Holy Cross fathers at St. Joseph's for their efforts to educate young Acadian men and prepare them to take an active role in Canadian society.

Around this time, Alice fell in love with an American, named Ovila Breau, who also had an Acadian heritage. She asked Léonard to be the best man and Roméo to be an usher at their wedding. Roméo was in a panic because he had no black shoes for the ceremony and no money to buy a pair. One of the priests at St. Joseph's came to the rescue and lent him a pair of his own shoes. Roméo stood proudly at the ceremony when Alice, his accomplice in so many tricks on the farm, was married.

After more months of hard study, Roméo graduated *cum laude* with his Bachelor of Arts degree, *Belles-Lettres*. He was right near the top in most subjects and, to his surprise, won an award for the student who worked hardest for the advancement of the French language. Gone were the days when he'd made thirty-two spelling and grammar mistakes!

Roméo was honoured by his fellow students when they chose him to be the valedictorian for the graduating class. He planned to deliver the speech in French and stayed up all night working on it. With no sleep and no breakfast, he arrived at the morning Convocation where a large crowd had gathered for the ceremony. Roméo felt a bit light-headed when he reached the podium, and before he could start his speech, he fell flat on the floor in a faint! He recovered and scrambled to his feet, feeling very embarrassed. He had to get through the speech, and he did.

Roméo's proud family, who had all made sacrifices for him, gathered around to congratulate him. It was June of 1948 and Roméo was 20 years old. His future lay a long way from the quiet Memramcook Valley.

Roméo at his university graduation

CHAPTER 6
OUT IN THE WORLD

Wearing a thirty-six-dollar suit bought from Eaton's, Roméo boarded a train just a few weeks after he graduated. He was headed for Montréal in Quebec, a province closer to the centre of Canada, where people also spoke French. He had a job as an editor with a student paper *La Vie étudiante*. The pay was low, but Roméo loved his first taste of life as a journalist.

A phone call in the middle of the year changed Roméo's future. His brother Léonard had been in a terrible car accident. It was February; the weather was cold, and the roads were icy. Léonard had been getting chains out of the trunk to put on the car. A second car came from behind, skidded and pinned him to the back of his car.

Léonard was taken by ambulance to the hospital, where they found he had broken legs and a crushed pelvic bone. He was so badly injured that even after weeks of recuperation he'd never again be able to do heavy farm work.

Roméo felt very far away and was worried about Léonard and his family. There were many medical expenses, and a man had to be hired to take over Léonard's farm duties. Roméo had to do something to help, but it wouldn't be working on the farm. He thought he should return to New Brunswick and find a job that paid more than his job in Montréal.

Looking around, Roméo saw that school teachers earned a good salary, so he decided to return to college to become a teacher. After a year of study, Roméo graduated and was hired to teach high school in a town in northern New Brunswick. He earned the large sum of $2,150 a year and sent most of it back to help with family expenses.

It was here that Roméo discovered his love of teaching. He was popular with students, teaching them history and French. He had been assigned to teach chemistry, but had unfortunately caused an explosion during an experiment, something former students talked about for years.

Roméo thought it was wrong that high school classes were all taught in English, when most of the students spoke French. He worked with his fellow teachers to change the system so French-speaking students could study and write their exams in French.

Roméo was good at communicating—with his readers when he wrote for newspapers, and with his students when he was teaching. He decided to make a film telling people in other parts of Canada about the dikes and locks from his childhood at Cormier's Cove.

Roméo was the writer and
Roger Blais was the director
of a film called *Les Aboiteaux*, made
with the National Film Board in 1955.

Whenever he could, Roméo returned to the farm and Mélindé's good home cooking. Mélindé and Antoine now had four children. Léonard could not do much hard work around the farm and was often cranky from constant pain. Roméo did his best to pitch in and help with the chores.

One day Roméo learned he'd had been awarded a scholarship by the Canadian government. The France-Acadie scholarship was a grant for one year of study in Paris.

Paris! The centre of Europe and the land his ancestors had left in the seventeenth century to come to Canada.

- STUDYING IN EUROPE -

Roméo was a twenty-six-year-old from a small Acadian village on his way to study in France. It was unbelievably exciting to think about living in the heart of Paris and being a student at the famous Sorbonne University. Roméo sailed from the city of Québec on the R.M.S. *Franconia*.

On board the ship there were lots of young people with dances and parties every night. One night a girl invited Roméo along with others to her cabin, where Roméo made the mistake of opening the porthole and letting sea water splash into the cabin. He was never invited again.

When he arrived in Paris, Roméo moved into the residence for Canadian students on campus, *La Maison canadienne*. He had decided to study techniques for teaching the French language, and began to work toward the highest degree, a doctorate.

It was an exciting time to be in Paris. Roméo ate in the little cafés on the Left Bank and came to love the baguettes, the wine, and the French people. New French novels were coming out, and he spent many evenings enjoying music, film, and theatre.

It was the custom for wealthy families in France to invite foreign students for Christmas dinner. In his first year Roméo was invited for chicken dinner with a French family, and, thinking of his two hungry roommates, he stuffed extra chicken legs in his jacket pocket. Unfortunately, he was caught and told to leave the house. Back at the college, he pulled the sticky chicken legs out of his pocket and gave them to his friends. They were hungry enough to be grateful for the messy treat.

Whenever he had a chance, Roméo travelled by train around Europe. He saw ancient ruins in Greece, fishing villages in Portugal, and watched the Pope speak to crowds in Rome. He fell in love with London.

Roméo's professor was pleased with his work and put his name forward for another scholarship. Before long Roméo learned he'd been awarded a scholarship from the Royal Society of Canada for a second year of study in Paris.

Roméo was working on his doctoral thesis in the spring of his second year when he heard very sad news from home. His oldest brother Antoine had been diagnosed with a brain tumour. Antoine died a few months later at the age of thirty-nine.

Roméo was needed in Canada. Abandoning his plans for a doctorate, he left Paris.

- TEACHING, AGAIN -

Antoine's wife Mélindé and their six children were all living at the LeBlanc farm with Philéas and Léonard. There were many medical expenses for Antoine's treatment before he died, and money was needed to hire yet another farm worker to take the place of hard-working Antoine.

Roméo decided he could earn good money working at what he was trained to do, so he applied for a job at the New Brunswick Normal School, a teacher training college in Fredericton, two hundred kilometers away from the farm.

Roméo was tall and good-looking, and, once again became a very popular teacher. He lectured the students about teaching French language and literature, and he earned what was then a good salary of $3,900 a year.

One of his first assignments was to ask students to write an essay about their elementary school experience. He wanted them to appreciate the importance of their introduction to learning, no doubt fondly remembering Miss Blanchet and his happy school days around the big coal stove.

One of his students was Germaine, a shy seventeen-year-old girl from Memramcook who had come to Fredericton to take the teacher's course. After the first week Germaine was homesick and announced to Roméo she was not coming back. Roméo suggested he could give her a ride back to Memramcook on the weekend. What Germaine remembers is that Roméo had a talk with her mother, her mother had a talk with her, and Sunday night Germaine surprised herself by returning to the college with Roméo. Looking back, she was always grateful to Roméo for changing her life. Germaine became a teacher and then a beloved school principal for thirty-five years!

Partway through his four years at the college, New Brunswick had a Commemoration celebrating two hundred years since the deportation of the Acadian people. Almost forty percent of the population of New Brunswick were French-speaking Acadians. They had not forgotten the courage of the early Acadians at the time of the deportation.

Roméo was now a widely travelled and well-educated young man who took great pride in his strong roots as an Acadian. New and very different adventures lay ahead.

ACADIAN CULTURE

Acadians are very proud of their 400-year-old history. Every year they honour their rich culture with a festival called *Tintamarre*.

Since 1881, August 15th has been celebrated as National Acadian Day with community events, parades, and outdoor concerts.

There is a saying that Acadians have "songs in their veins and music in their fingertips." Suzie LeBlanc and other performers have revived traditional songs, and church and school choirs are known for their excellent performances. The new generation of singers like Lisa LeBlanc and The Hay Babies have gained international recognition.

One of the most famous Acadian authors is Antonine Maillet, who has written a novel entitled *Pélagie-la-Charette* (about an Acadian widow's return from exile), and a play, the touching story of the life of a poor but wise Acadian cleaning woman, entitled *La Sagouine*.

Acadians are proud of their blue, white, and red flag with a gold star, the colours based on the flag of France, where their ancestors set sail for the new world. They visit the town of Memramcook, called "the cradle of new Acadie," and the historical village of Bertrand where visitors see people in traditional dress, living in traditional houses. They celebrate with their favourite Acadian foods like chicken *fricot* and *poutine râpée*.

Along with tourists, Acadians make the pilgrimage to see the elegant statue of Evangeline near the shore of Grand-Pré, Nova Scotia. Grand-Pré is the port where many expelled Acadians were loaded onto ships and forced to leave their homeland.

Some Canadians believe the first French settlers came to live in Quebec, but Acadians have not forgotten that the first French settlements were in the beautiful valleys near the sea in the Maritimes.

CHAPTER 7
NEW HORIZONS IN THE POLITICAL WORLD

Roméo thought he'd like to try his hand at journalism, something he'd been interested in since his university days. He still remembered the bulletin board at St. Joseph's where students crowded around to read page one and two of *Le Devoir* posted in the morning and pages three and four in the afternoon.

Roméo applied for a job as political correspondent with *Radio-Canada*, the French half of the Canadian Broadcasting Corporation. He was hired and moved to London, England. It felt as though he was at the centre of the world, living in London and sending breaking news back to Canada. One day, doing his washing in a laundromat, he made friends with a Canadian girl named Lyn Carter, who was also working in London.

After two years in London, Roméo was transferred to Washington, D.C., where he reported on difficult American issues including the war in Vietnam. During that time Roméo re-united with Lyn, and they were married. A whole new life opened up for Roméo: he was a family man now, and about to change the direction of his career.

- INTO POLITICAL LIFE -

So far in his adult life, Roméo had always been an observer who reported what he saw, but he'd never been a part of political life. In 1967, he was offered the job of press secretary to Prime Minister Lester Pearson, a job which put him at the centre of Ottawa politics.

Roméo was a great admirer of Prime Minister Pearson, leader of the Liberal Party and winner of the Nobel Peace Prize. As his press secretary, Roméo became the person who explained to the public what Prime Minister Pearson's Liberal government was doing. These were busy years: a new Canadian flag was chosen, and the Separatist movement was gaining strength, with the French in Quebec calling for their independence. Roméo shared a passion for baseball with the Prime Minister, and often the two of them escaped from work to watch the Montréal Expos play a game.

Roméo became a father two years later when his son Dominic was born on the very same day Lester Pearson resigned from his job. Roméo should have been at the Mr. Pearson's side for the announcement, instead of in the hospital with Lyn, holding his new baby. *The Montreal* Star reported that Lester Pearson joked, "Wherefore art thou, Roméo?"

Roméo responded by saying, "Today I lost a prime minister but gained a son!"

Pierre Trudeau became the next leader of the Liberal Party and Canada's Prime Minister. He'd seen how good Roméo was at his job and asked him to stay on as press secretary. Trudeau won a majority in the next election, and Roméo worked at his side for the next two exciting years.

At the end of that time Roméo decided to leave Ottawa and return to live in the Maritimes. He'd bought an old converted convent that included a chapel, located at Grande-Digue on the Northumberland Strait, close to the Gulf of St. Lawrence. The cottage provided an escape from the busy political world.

But once again, Roméo would find a new challenge with an unexpected turn in his life.

- A JUMP INTO PARLIAMENT -

Roméo wasn't away from Ottawa for long. Friends in Ottawa and in New Brunswick kept urging him to run for election as a member of parliament. He thought about it for weeks, before deciding to take the big step. He'd be a Liberal candidate in the riding of Westmorland-Kent, later Beauséjour, on the eastern coast of the New Brunswick.

Roméo was a refreshing kind of political candidate. During the campaign he insisted on carrying his own suitcase, and rather than speaking at large political rallies, he held what he called "kitchen meetings" where he could talk to people in their own homes. Many of the people in his riding earned their living fishing, and Roméo was a good listener when fishermen told him about their problems.

Everyone in the community liked Roméo, and in 1972 he was elected with a big majority. He headed back to Ottawa, this time as an MP, a Member of Parliament. For four years he was busy with House of Commons sittings, committee meetings, and frequent trips back to his riding in New Brunswick. During those years Roméo and Lyn had a second child, a daughter they named Geneviève.

Living in Ottawa, Roméo was pleased to have an old friend as a new neighbour. Laurianne, his elementary school classmate, had married a man in the Air Force, and they were living in Ottawa. One day Laurianne decided to cook pudding in a bag, Roméo's favourite childhood dish, and she called Roméo to come for dinner. The delicious dessert and the talk of the old days at Cormier's Cove were welcome break in the midst of their busy lives.

In 1976 Prime Minister Trudeau recognized Roméo's political skills and awarded him a cabinet post, appointing him Minister of Fisheries and Oceans. The fishermen in New Brunswick loved the man they called The Codfather and knew they could count on him to fight for their fishing rights.

"Don't call me minister of fish," Roméo insisted. "Call me minister of fisherman!"

Roméo with his young children Geneviève and Dominic

Roméo's major accomplishment was to set a two-hundred-mile fishing limit off the Atlantic and Pacific coasts, and later the Arctic ocean. The new limit protected Canadian fish by keeping other nations from fishing inside Canadian waters.

These were busy times for Roméo. The Liberal government passed the important Canadian Charter of Rights and Freedoms during those years. He was away from home a great deal and worked long hours. The demands of political life are often a strain on a family, and Roméo's marriage to Lyn ended at that time. They shared caring for Dominic who was fourteen and Geneviève who was nine.

In our parliamentary democracy the laws that govern us are decided by the House of Commons which is made up of members from a political party (or an Independent) elected to represent the country. Every citizen over the age of eighteen is allowed to vote in the elections held every four years. The candidate who wins the most votes in a constituency becomes a Member of Parliament (MP) and will have a seat in the House of Commons in Ottawa.

The House of Commons

The party winning the most seats will form the Government. The party with the second highest number of seats forms the Opposition. The House of Commons meets throughout the year to debate and vote on bills that become the laws governing the country.

Cabinet Ministers (up to 40) appointed by the Prime Minister to govern all areas of the country, like the environment, finance, immigration, fisheries and foreign affairs.

The **Prime Minister** chosen by the party with the most seats

The **Senate** can have up to 105 members. The members and the Senate Leader are not elected, but are selected by the Prime Minister and his advisors. Their role is to discuss and review the bills passed by the House of Commons. If they approve, the new laws are sent to the Governor General for final approval.

The **Governor General,** as the Queen's representative, gives royal assent to laws passed by Parliarnent.

36 million
population of Canada

/

338 number
of constituencies

/

Political Parties
Liberal
Conservative
New Democratic
Green
Bloc québécois

- UP THE LADDER -

Prime Minister Trudeau had great respect for Roméo's reputation for fairness, honesty and hard work. It was a surprise and an honour when the prime minister appointed fifty-seven-year-old Roméo to the upper house of Parliament, called the Senate.

Roméo plunged into the new work, dealing with Quebec's demand to become a distinct society, and, most notably, welcoming refugees who came by boat to the shores of the Atlantic provinces. He made certain that refugee families were given enough food, shelter, and clothing to begin their new life in Canada.

At this time, Jean Chrétien became the new Liberal Party leader. He was aware that Roméo was well-liked, was a good listener and a hard worker. Prime Minister Chrétien rewarded Roméo with an appointment as Speaker of the Senate. Roméo's job was to keep order in the Senate debates and see that bills from the House of Commons were fairly debated.

While he was Speaker, Roméo married Diana Fowler, who had been his friend for many years. Diana was with Roméo when Prime Minister Chrétien called one night to offer Roméo the highest position in the land.

THE ROLE OF THE GOVERNOR GENERAL OF CANADA

Canada is a parliamentary democracy and a constitutional monarchy. This means Canada is governed by an elected parliament with its own constitution. It also means that Her Majesty Queen Elizabeth II is Queen of Canada (and of the United Kingdom, of course), with the Governor General as her official representative.

At Canada's Confederation on July 1, 1867, Queen Victoria chose an Englishman, Viscount Monck, to be the first Governor General of Canada. In 1952, the Prime Minister appointed the first Canadian citizen, the popular Vincent Massey, to the position.

It is important to remember that this is an appointed position, not an elected one. The term is traditionally five years but may be shortened or extended. There is a tradition of alternating francophone and anglophone nominees. Most appointments have been to men, but several women have served in that position: Jeanne Sauvé, Adrienne Clarkson, Michaëlle Jean, and our new Governor General, Her Excellency the Right Honourable Julie Payette.

The Governor General is paid an annual salary and given residences at Rideau Hall in Ottawa and La Citadelle in the city of Québec.

The Governor General plays an important role after an election to call upon an elected leader with the confidence of Parliament to form the government. The Governor General presides over the swearing-in of the Prime Minister, the chief justice of Canada and cabinet ministers. At the opening of Parliament, the Governor General reads the Speech from the Throne outlining the government's agenda. The Governor General has the rights to be consulted, to encourage and to warn the government in place. A bill passed by the House of Commons and the Senate does not become law until it receives royal assent through the Governor General's signature.

The Governor General is the official host to the Queen and visiting heads of State from other countries and travels to represent Canada around the world.

The Governor General presides over ceremony investitures for the Order of Canada, the most prestigious honour for outstanding achievement in Canada, as well as over the presentations of awards given in visual and literary arts. The Governor General's Literary Awards include categories for children's literature and illustrations, as well as categories for fiction, nonfiction, poetry, drama and translation, in French and English.

CHAPTER 8
THE GOVERNOR GENERAL OF CANADA

In that phone call, Prime Minister Jean Chrétien asked Roméo if he would accept the position of governor general of Canada.

This invitation was a complete surprise to Roméo. He felt he was just an ordinary man, born into a New Brunswick Acadian community a long way from Ottawa. Why was *he* asked to be the Queen's representative in Canada? It was the highest honour in the country! And there had never been an Acadian governor general before.

When Roméo expressed doubts, Prime Minister Chrétien insisted Roméo was the right man for the job. He had the qualities and experience that made him the perfect choice. Roméo knew he had experience on the political scene, but he'd been looking forward to retirement at his cottage at Grande-Digue. He discussed the possibility of such a big change with Diana. It *would* be a big change, one he never expected, but it was also an honour. He decided to accept.

Three months later Roméo, accompanied by Diana, travelled to England to be officially appointed by Queen Elizabeth II as her representative in Canada. They were invited to stay overnight with the royal family at Sandringham House. At the formal dinner the first night, the queen, Prince Philip, Prince Charles, Princess Anne, and the Queen Mother sat around the large dining room table. Always comfortable in any situation, Roméo chatted with the Royals and got on famously with the Queen Mother. The Queen's lively Welsh Corgis kept them company under the table.

As servers brought the first plate, Roméo saw a row of green peas sitting on an endive leaf. Just then the Queen announced proudly that the peas had been grown in the palace greenhouse. Diana shot Roméo a look. She knew that ever since he was a child Roméo couldn't stand green peas. But they were dining with the Queen of England. Roméo ate the peas!

Well past midnight, the queen presented Roméo and Diana with the insignia of Companion of the Order of Canada. Roméo was now all set to assume his responsabilities as her representative in Canada. Such a simple act; so many new challenges ahead.

- A NEW RESIDENCE -

Back in Ottawa Roméo and Diana moved into Government House, known as Rideau Hall, the official residence of the governor general.

From the beginning, the staff could see that Roméo was a different kind of governor general. When he was offered a military uniform as Commander-in-Chief of the Canadian Armed Forces, Roméo refused to wear it. "I haven't fought in any war," he told them. He didn't feel he had a right to wear a military uniform or any medals.

The installation ceremony for Roméo was held on February 8, 1995. Roméo's father was no longer living but his brother Léonard and his nephew Charles travelled to Ottawa for the event. Roméo, aged 68, was named His Excellency the Right Honorable Roméo Adrien LeBlanc, Canada's 25th governor general, the first from the Atlantic provinces, and the first Acadian.

"I don't think I can call my little brother His Excellency," Léonard said, but Leonard was as proud as anyone of the boy who'd been scared of a bull on the farm.

In his installation speech Roméo talked about how his village in New Brunswick was his world. "My world was French and Catholic," he said. "The next door world was English and Protestant." Two very different cultures, he explained, but whenever there was trouble, a barn burned down or a field flooded, they pulled together to help each other. "Then there was a war…. and we died together, not as English or French speaking, but as Canadians," Roméo proudly told the audience assembled for the ceremony.

THE STANLEY CUP

From 1888 until 1893, Lord Frederick Arthur Stanley was Governor General. In the winter his sons and his one daughter loved to play the popular street or ice hockey known as "shinny."

For many years, stick-and-ball games had been played by the Mi'kmaq First Nations communities in Nova Scotia. Then, British soldiers brought sticks and balls with them when they came to Canada and quickly adapted them to play on ice.

Lord Stanley's daughter, Isobel, was one of the first women to play ice hockey, and in 1892 Lord Stanley decided to recognize the game with an award. He donated a silver cup as a trophy. To this day, we all know it as the Stanley Cup which is awarded to the best professional hockey team in North America.

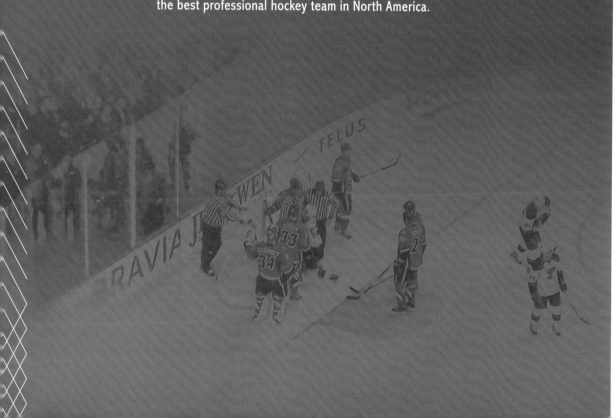

- A MAN OF THE PEOPLE -

Roméo's first official visit as governor general was back to New Brunswick, to the place where he had grown up and still had many family members. It was a big event for the small Cormier's Cove and Memramcook communities. Owners painted their houses, and yards were tidied up to welcome their own Acadian boy. Roméo was touched to see how proud the people were to have one of their own as the governor general of Canada.

In February 1996, Roméo presided at the opening of Parliament back in Ottawa. Roméo sat, with Diana beside him, before the members of the Senate and the House of Commons to read the government's Speech from the Throne.

Roméo reading the Speech from the Throne, 1996, with Diana

Roméo began to make changes. He believed that people across Canada should know more about the governor general's role, and he wanted them to feel welcome in Rideau Hall. After all, it belongs to the people of Canada, he said.

Roméo set up a Visitor Centre in an old building on the grounds of Rideau Hall and expanded tours to include the state dining room, the drawing room, his personal, the greenhouses and the private gardens. There were activities for children in an activity centre tent beside a playground.

Rideau Hall hosted tobogganing and skating parties every winter, summer concerts, children's Christmas parties and even a teddy bear picnic on the grounds. With Roméo and Diana's welcoming attitude, visitors to the governor general's residence grew to thousands every year.

Those were exciting years. The queen and royal family members made three visits, and once again, Roméo did things his way. He'd never liked long formal dining tables used for state occasions. He asked his staff to set up round tables, so guests could talk to each other. There was another surprise for the queen, who was delighted when she saw an outdoor barbecue and a buffet table where guests could help themselves.

Roméo with Nelson Mandela and Prime Minister Jean Chrétien, 1998

The LeBlancs had visits from the U.S. President Bill Clinton, King Hussein of Jordan, and President Nelson Mandela of South Africa. And there were trips around the world. In Africa and India, Roméo and Diana brought gifts of children's books and farm implements donated by Canadians.

Diana accompanied Roméo as they travelled across Canada, visiting big cities, farming towns, and isolated villages. Whenever they could, Roméo and Diana asked to spend time with children in schools and hospitals.

In his time as governor general, Roméo gave over eight hundred speeches. He talked about First Nations people and how we must respect their equality along with their differences. He proclaimed June 21st National Aboriginal Day, saying, "Many cities in Canada are less than a hundred years old. But Aboriginal people have lived in this land for more than a hundred centuries."

He had a totem pole carved by Mungo Martin of the Kwakiutl Nation placed at the front of the Rideau Hall grounds, along with an inuksuk unveiled on the second National Aboriginal Day in 1997.

THE CARING CANADIAN AWARD

In 2015, the Caring Canadian Award established by Roméo LeBlanc transformed, with the approval of The Queen, into a national honour called the Sovereign's Medal for Volunteers.

In establishing the award in 1995, Roméo wanted to honour the thousands of volunteers who have enriched the lives of every Canadian and asked nothing for themselves.

In his own words: "Let us recognize the parents who daily nurture their developmentally challenged children ... Let us recognize the children who care for parents struck down by an unrelenting illness such as Alzheimer's disease.... (and) single parents, who, in the face of great economic and social difficulties, raise children to be successful adults..."

Any Canadian can submit the name of volunteers in their community to an advisory committee which makes the final selection. The Medal for Volunteers is presented to recipients at honours ceremonies across the country.

At a Canada Day speech on Parliament Hill July 1, 1998, Roméo spoke about Canada as a proud multicultural country. He talked about the immigrants and refugees who have always been welcome in Canada. "They come to this country," he said, "with nothing but their hands and their hopes. It is through hard work that people from many lands have flourished in their adopted country."

In 1999 His Excellency signed the proclamation for the creation of Canada's new territory of Nunavut.

- RECOGNIZING ORDINARY PEOPLE -

Roméo knew that as governor general he had "the right to be consulted, the right to warn, and the right to encourage." To him, the most important of these was the right to encourage.

Roméo felt strongly there should be an award for the hard work and dedication of ordinary people. For years, the prestigious Order of Canada had been given to honour outstanding achievements by accomplished Canadians. But Roméo knew that every day there were men and women volunteers and caregivers also making valuable contributions in their own communities. He decided to set up an award called the governor general's Caring Canadian Award.

One of the first awards was given to a single immigrant woman who had eight children of her own. When she heard about three handicapped children in need of a home, she adopted them, adding them to her family. In his time as governor general, Roméo presented the Caring Canadian award to almost 500 volunteers and caregivers such as this woman in ceremonies across the country.

Roméo made another change too. He remembered his own years of teaching high school. He knew how hard it was to be a good teacher, and often said that teaching history was the most important work he ever did. Now, as governor general, he wanted to inspire and reward teachers, so he established the Governor General's Award for Excellence in Teaching Canadian History. It recognized inspired teachers and historians who bring history to life in new ways. One of the first recipients was a teacher from Manitoba who encouraged her students to use music and role playing to perform plays about social activists like Louis Riel and Nellie McClung.

- ROMÉO NEVER FORGOT HIS FAMILY -

Throughout the busy years, Roméo always kept in touch with his family. "Some people in an important position will forget their family," Leonard said, "but not Roméo."

Roméo helped by sending money for his nieces and nephews to have their teeth fixed, for books and glasses and school trips. He bought a house for Léonard, who had never married and still had pain from the accident and needed to walk with a cane.

Roméo liked to spend as much time as he could in the summer in the cottage at Grande-Digue. One year he organized a reunion of ninety-five relatives spanning four generations. It was a happy pot-luck picnic overlooking the sea.

During his years as governor general, Roméo escaped every spring to travel to Florida to watch his favourite baseball team, the Montreal Expos, at their spring training. His executive assistant said that it would be putting it mildly to call Roméo a baseball fanatic! He was right.

Once, during the U.S. ambassador's visit to the Citadel, the official Quebec residence of the queen and the governor general, the staff thought the two men were inside the room discussing important political issues. How could they have guessed that the ambassador and Roméo were enthusiastically talking about which baseball team should win the current series!

Just before Roméo retired, his sisters and their families came to visit at Rideau Hall. Nine of them laughed and reminisced together about their early life and feasted on the wonderful Acadian food they all loved.

Roméo at a baseball game, 1996

As they hugged goodbye, Roméo noticed that his sister Alice seemed quiet. Sadly, on the trip home, Alice died of a heart attack. It was very upsetting for Roméo to lose the sister who had always been so much fun. Speaking at her funeral, he recounted the old days on the farm when they were both young, and how she had taught him to get out of work by pulling up the new carrot shoots instead of the weeds. How Léonard was furious and said he'd never let them loose in the garden again, which was just what he and Alice wanted. It had given Roméo a chance to sneak away with his book and read the rest of the day.

After almost five years as governor general, Roméo was 72 years old and tired. He announced that he was retiring from office. He and Diana took the train from Ottawa to New Brunswick. It was touching to see big crowds of people in Ottawa waving good-bye, and to be welcomed home by even larger crowds in New Brunswick. It was the right decision to make.

The official portrait of Roméo LeBlanc by Christan Nicholson hangs in Rideau Hall.

CHAPTER 9
RETIREMENT

Some people expected Roméo and Diana to stay in Ottawa when he stepped down as governor general. But anyone who knew Roméo knew he longed to return to his real home, the cottage at Grande-Digue.

He loved that coast, not too far from the wide Bay of Fundy where the tides would swamp the flat marshes near his childhood home. And his cottage was not far from St. Joseph's College, the place where his sister Émilie changed his life forever when she gave him the chance to get more education.

But Roméo had one more responsibility in Ottawa. The staff continually reminded him that he had not returned to have his official portrait painted. Large gilt-framed portraits of the former governors general lined the walls of Rideau Hall, and there was an empty space for Roméo's official portrait. An artist from New Brunswick had been selected and Roméo needed to return to Ottawa one more time.

*Dominic LeBlanc being sworn in as a member of parliament
with his father, mother, sister and the Clerk of the House of Commons, 2000*

Roméo didn't like the idea of posing for a formal portrait so he kept putting off the trip. Finally a day was set, and a reluctant Roméo packed his suitcase and left New Brunswick for Ottawa with Diana. They arrived at Rideau Hall and went to meet the artist, Christan Nicholson, who was to paint the official portrait. As they gathered for the sitting, Diana pointed out that Roméo's suit jacket and pants didn't match.

No one knew quite what to do about the mismatch until the painter, who was dressed as a casual working artist, offered Roméo his sweater. Roméo, who wasn't keen on wearing a suit anyway, quickly agreed.

And so, the official portrait of Canada's 25th governor general shows a very relaxed Roméo Adrien LeBlanc, arms folded, wearing a borrowed and rather baggy grey sweater lent to him by a friendly artist.

It is a portrait that shows the humble nature of this man from a small Acadian village, a man who cared more about his fellow Canadians than how he was dressed.

Happily back at his beloved cottage, Roméo enjoyed entertaining visitors. He would put on his baseball cap and proudly show off the tomatoes and gooseberries growing in his garden. Now and then he'd slip down to the local bakery for the treat of a sticky bun. Every year without fail, Roméo made the Christmas puddings.

With a habit left over from his days working for the press, Roméo read six newspapers a day, adding them to the stacks of papers piled in every corner of the cottage.

Roméo had the satisfaction of seeing his son Dominic elected as a member of the House of Commons, representing Roméo's old riding of Beauséjour, and taking his place in the centre of government in Ottawa.

There were always visits from his two children, his brother Léonard, his nieces and nephews and old friends. Sometimes his schoolmate of long ago, Laurianne, dropped by for a visit, and the two of them shared memories of their school days.

Roméo's favourite time to walk along the shore was when the sea was calm. In the late afternoons with the sun low in the sky and the sea birds circling, Roméo's heart was full of memories: memories of the farm in Cormier's Cove, his school days at St. Joseph's, the carefree years in Paris and London, the exciting times in politics with three prime ministers, and his later years as the Queen's representative.

Roméo died peacefully at home at the age of 81.

The state funeral for Roméo was held in Saint Thomas Church in Memramcook and was attended by many politicians and dignitaries. Lining the route from the town were local fishermen who knew Roméo as their member of parliament, and villagers who remembered him as a boy growing up and walking to school in their village.

During the twenty-one-gun salute at the cemetery, the midday CNR train passed by, giving a haunting whistle that echoed in tribute through the valley.

At the door to the reception, two young RCMP officers checked a list of invited guests but were unable to stop the older village men and women from entering. These people had known Roméo all their lives and were determined to be part of the event. The old-timers gathered inside to reminisce about Roméo with stories, jokes, and pranks from his childhood. They had a deep love for one of their own who had not forgotten his roots.

One of the villagers proudly told a reporter, "Roméo's a good man. He's one of us."

Roméo LeBlanc lived a full and satisfying life. He was an inspiring example of a man who stayed true to his humble Acadian origins, even while he served the highest office of the land.

Roméo by the shore at Grande-Digue

CHAPTER 10
THE LEGACY OF GOVERNOR GENERAL ROMÉO LEBLANC

Roméo Le Blanc died in 2009, leaving behind a quiet but enduring legacy.

Roméo wanted visitors from Canada and abroad to feel welcome in Rideau Hall. With more access to buildings and a children's activity centre, the grounds attracted thousands of visitors who came every year to learn about the role of the Queen's representative in Canada.

Dear to Roméo's heart was the Caring Canadian Award, now officially transformed into the Sovereign's Medal for Volunteers. Since Roméo LeBlanc's time in office, over 4,000 volunteers have received this honour in ceremonies across the country.

He also established the Governor General's Award for Excellence in Teaching Canadian History. Every year members of the National History Society choose historians and school teachers from each province to receive awards for the innovative teaching and writing of history.

One of Roméo's major accomplishments came from the time he was Minister of Fisheries. He fought for the rights of fishermen and established the two-hundred-mile fishing limit off three Canadian coasts. The fishing limit stands to this day.

Most importantly, the Acadian community feels a sense of pride in themselves, their history and their contribution to Canada.

As a postscript it is fitting to acknowledge that Roméo's contribution to his country has been recognized in recent times. In 2010, Canada Post issued a postage stamp in his honour, and in 2016 the University of Moncton established the Roméo LeBlanc Scholarship Fund for the Advancement of Excellence in Journalism. It gives generous financial support to third and fourth year journalism students and reflects Roméo's own career beginnings in journalism. In the same year the airport in New Brunswick was renamed the Greater Moncton Roméo LeBlanc International airport.

And so the memory of Roméo LeBlanc lives on in the daily lives of Canadians.

ROMÉO LEBLANC
1927–2009

CANADA 57

APPENDICES

AUTHOR'S NOTE

I met Roméo LeBlanc in 2002. His first wife Lyn took me to stay at Grande-Digue, in his cottage on the shore of the Northumberland Strait in New Brunswick. Roméo had been retired for a few years and had a reputation for being friendly. Sure enough, he was gracious and welcoming. I was charmed.

He announced that he'd cook a feast of lobster for us, and he did. After supper I walked with him down to the shore where we stood side by side looking out across the strait. I could see he was a man at ease: a man content with his life.

Lyn and I stayed overnight in his cottage where the solitary bedrooms formerly occupied by nuns were set out in a row down the narrow hallway.

The next morning, I had a jar of Roméo's gooseberry jam on the seat beside me as Lyn drove me the short distance to Memramcook to see the farm house where Roméo was born, and where his eighty-year-old sister-in-law, Mélindé, still lived. While we walked around the village, Lyn told me the story of how Roméo had not been allowed to go to high school until his sister paid his tuition out of her maid's salary.

I remember thinking that Roméo's childhood would make a good story for children, never dreaming that one day I would write it myself.

Roméo died a few years after my visit, and more than ten years had gone by since I again thought of writing this book. It may seem strange that a children's writer living in British Columbia would want to write about a person from the other side of Canada, but I felt Roméo's story was one all Canadians can be proud of.

Researching the book for almost three years I've met Roméo's second wife, Diana, his children, Dominic and Gen, and several of his relatives. I've been again to the farm house where he grew up and stood in the bedroom where he slept, held the school books he loved and talked to three women in their nineties who knew Roméo as a boy. They've told me many stories about the man they greatly admired.

In writing a biography of Roméo's life, I have added dialogue along with actual quotes to bring his experiences to life for readers.

Back in New Brunswick along the research road, I've learned much about Acadian history and culture, and also met many wonderful Acadians who have helped with the research for this book. They have now become my friends.

ACKNOWLEDGEMENTS

I have many people to thank for help with this book.

First, I want to thank Roméo's family: Lyn LeBlanc for introducing me to Roméo many years ago, Roméo's children Dominic and Geneviève for supporting this project, and Diana Fowler LeBlanc for generously sharing memories and photographs and for introducing me to other members of the family. Roméo's nephew Charles and his wife Cécile kindly drove me to the old homestead in Memramcook and introduced me to Mélindé who was a big part of Roméo's childhood. They also introduced to me the best lobster roll I've ever eaten. Linda Breau-Norman, Roméo's niece who lives in the U.S., shared many memories of her uncle.

From the beginning, I had strong support from Robert Pichette who was a good friend and a speech writer for Roméo LeBlanc, as well as the inspired translator of this book. I am very grateful for his enthusiasm, his dedicated hard work, and our friendship.

In writing this book, I had the mentoring support of Debbie Hodge. Debbie writes the kind of books I admire and understands the kind of story I want to tell. She is a skilled and insightful guide, generous with her time and gentle in her ways.

It was my lucky day when Jean A. Gaudet at the Société d'histoire de

Memramcook answered my first email query. Hundreds of questions and emails and two years later when Jean had patiently researched many details for me, I travelled to New Brunswick and met Jean. He kindly drove me around Memramcook and I fell in love with the beautiful valley, the amazing tidal rivers and the Acadian people in the village.

Among my new Acadian friends, I especially want to thank Laurianne LeBlanc, who generously shared her memories of going to school with Roméo and being his friend for most of her ninety-three years. Rose-Anna LeBlanc and Germaine Poirier kindly told me about their time with Roméo.

For research help I am grateful to Jocelyne LeBlanc, New Brunswick Public Library in Memramcook; Martin Lanther, Library and Archives Canada; Maurice Basque and François LeBlanc, Centre of Acadian Studies, Université de Moncton; Joanne Duguay, Moncton Museum and Transportation Discovery Centre; Bernard Portier; Harvey Barkun; Jeannette Gaudet Boudreau; Huberte Gaudet; Claude Boudreau; Eddie St. Pierre; Emma Lee Arsenault; Claude Bourque; André Léger; Ed Broadbent; Dr. Michael Teed; Béatrice Boudreau; Damien Cormier; Bernard Richard; Dr. John Wood, and to Dr. Naomi E. S. Griffiths, who kindly shared background from her fine biography *The Golden Age of Liberalism: a Portrait of Roméo LeBlanc.*

I want to thank the helpful women at the Government House: Heather Williamson, National Capital Commission, Marie-Pierre Bélanger, Fabienne Fusade and Marie Glinski of Rideau Hall.

Thanks to my supportive friends, many of whom are writers and all of whom are readers: Dianne Woodman, Norma Charles, Linda Bailey, Susan Moger, Leslie Buffam, Madeleine Nelson, Louise Hager, Danielle and Bob Marcotte, Don and Lydia Kasianchuk, Maureen Thackray, Glen Huser, Roberta Rich, Anne Fraser, Marc Bell, Lindsay Graham, Ron and Veronica Hatch, Monica Kulling, Mary Sanderson, Nancy Ennis, Jane Flick, Robert Heidbreder, Ed Broadbent, and Gillian Chetty.

And many thanks to Marie Cadieux and Sébastien Lord-Émard at Bouton d'or Acadie who have enthusiastically embraced this book, along with their talented editors, designers and illustrators: Jo-Anne Elder, Réjean Ouellette, Maurice Cormier, Romain Blanchard, and Isabelle Léger.

Loving thanks to my family who are as proud of me as I am of them.

I am grateful for financial support during the travel and research phase of this book from Access Copyright and the British Columbia Arts Council.

TIME LINE

EVENTS IN ROMÉO'S LIFE		EVENTS IN CANADA
Roméo is born December 18 in Cormier's Cove, N.B.	1927	1927 Mackenzie King is Prime Minister
		1929 The Great Depression begins
Roméo starts Grade 1	1933	
Roméo's mother dies	1935	1939 World War II begins
Roméo starts Grade 8	1940	1941 Joe DiMaggio sets new hitting record
Roméo graduates with B.A.	1944	1945 World War II ends
		1949 Newfoundland joins Canada
Roméo graduates with a B. Ed.	1951	
Roméo teaches high school in Drummond, N.B.	1951-53	
Roméo studies in Paris	1954-55	
Roméo teaches at N.B. Teacher's college	1955-59	
Roméo works for CBC radio in London, Washington and Ottawa	1960-67	
		1963-68 Lester Pearson is Prime Minister
		1965 Canada has a new maple leaf flag
		1967 Canada celebrates 100 years since Confederation
Roméo is press secretary to Prime Minister Pearson	1967-68	1968 Medicare is passed in Canada

Roméo's life	Year	Canadian history
	1969	N.B. makes both English and French official languages
Roméo is press secretary to Prime Minister Trudeau	1969-71	
	1969-79	Pierre Trudeau is Prime Minister
Roméo is director of Public Relations at L'Université de Moncton	1971-72	
Roméo is member of parliarment for Westmoland-Kent, N.B.	1972-84	
	1976	Canada announces 200 mile coastal fishing zone
Roméo is Minister of Fisheries and Environment	1974-82	
	1980	*Oh Canada* is adopted as official anthem
Roméo is Minister of Public Works	1982-84	
	1984	Jeanne Sauvé becomes Canada's first woman Governor General
Roméo is appointed to the Senate	1984	
	1984-93	Brian Mulroney is Prime Minister
Roméo is appointed Speaker of the Senate	1993	
	1993	Jean Chrétien is Prime Minister
Roméo is appointed Governor General of Canada by The Queen	1995	
	1995	The referendum on Quebec's separation is defeated
	1999	The territory of Nunavut is created
Roméo retires as Governor General	1999	
Roméo dies at Grande-Digue, N.B.	2009	

BOOKS AND RESSOURCES

▪ Books in French (Young Readers)

Le Trésor de Memramcook de Dominic Langlois, illustrations de Maurice Cormier, Bouton d'or Acadie

La Butte à Pétard de Diane Carmel Léger, Bouton d'or Acadie

L'Acadie en baratte : Petit guide inusité des Maritimes, de Diane Carmel Léger, Bouton d'or Acadie

Évangéline et Gabriel, Pauline Gill, Lanctôt Éditeur

▪ Books in English (Young Readers)

Winds of L'Acadie by Lois Donovan. Ronsdale Press

Dear Canada Series: Banished from Our Home: The Acadian Diary of Angélique Richard – Grand-Pré, Acadie 1755 by Sharon Stewart, Scholastic Canada

Piau's Potato Present by Diane Carmel Léger, Bouton d'or Acadie

Life in Acadia by Romemary Neering and Stan Garrod. Growth of a Nation Series, Fitzhenry and Whiteside Company

Evangeline for Young Readers by Helene Boudreau and Patsy Mackinnon. Nimbus Publishing

▪ Cookbooks

A Taste of Acadie by Marielle Cormier-Boudreau and Melvin Gallant (translated by Ernest Bauer), Goose Lane Editions

La Cuisine traditionnelle en Acadie by Marielle Cormier Boudreau et Melvin Gallant, Éditions de la Francophonie.

Acadian Pictorial Cookbook with photos by Wayne Barrett, Nimbus Publishing

Pantry and Palate: Remembering and Rediscovering Acadian Food, Simon Thibault, Nimbus Publishing

▪ Film

The National Film Board film *Les Aboiteaux* written by Roméo LeBlanc can be seen at www.onf.ca/film.aboiteaux

▪ Pamphlets

Dykes and Aboiteaux: the Acadians Turned Salt Marshes into Fertile Meadows, Société Promotion Grand-Pré

Les digues et les aboiteaux: Les Acadiens transforment les marais salés en prés fertiles, Société Promotion Grand-Pré

▪ Books for Adult Readers in English

Evangeline: a Tale of Acadie by Henry Wadsworth Longfellow, Goose Lane Editions

The Acadians of NS: Past and Present by Sally Ross and Alphonse Deveau, Nimbus Publishing Ltd.

The Contexts of Acadian History 1686-1784, by Naomi E.S. Griffiths, McGill University Press

The Golden Age of Liberalism; a Portrait of Roméo LeBlanc, by Naomi E.S. Griffiths, Lorimer and Company

A Great and Noble Scheme: The Tragic Story of the Expulsion of the French Acadians from Their American Homeland, by John Mack Faragher, W.W.Norton & Company Ltd.

▪ Books for Adult Readers in French

Histoire des Acadiens et des Acadiennes du Nouveau-Brunswick, de Sylvain Godin et Maurice Basque, Éditions de La Grande Marée

L'Acadie, hier et aujourd'hui, collectif dirigé par Phil Comeau, Waren Perrin et Mary Broussard Perrin, Éditions de La Grande Marée

Le pays appelé l'Acadie : réflexions sur des commémorations, de Robert Pichette. Centre d'études acadiennes de l'Université de Moncton

Histoire de l'Université de Moncton, Maurice Basque et Marc Robichaud, Institut d'études acadiennes

ILLUSTRATIONS AND PHOTOGRAPHY CREDITS

INDEX

Printed and bound in Canada by Transcontinental
2018, December.
for Bouton d'or Acadie, book publisher since 1996